HUNTING SCENES

Pictures of the Holderness Hunt

Edited by
JOHN MARKHAM

Highgate Publications (Beverley) Ltd 1989

Published by Highgate Publications (Beverley) Ltd.
24 Wylies Road, Beverley, North Humberside, HU17 7AP
Telephone (0482) 866826

Printed by
B.A. Press, 2-4 Newbegin, Lairgate, Beverley, HU17 8EG
Telephone (0482) 882232

© John Markham 1989

British Library Cataloguing in Publication Data

Hunting Scenes: pictures of the Holderness Hunt.
 1. Humberside. Holderness (District). Foxes. Hunting — Hunts, history.
I Markham, John.
799.2'5974442

ISBN 0-948929-20-0

Editor's Note

Most of the photographs in the collection have no caption. As many as possible have been identified and in this intriguing but difficult task David and Sue Neave, Jill Crowther, Sarah Goodrick, Jennifer Stanley, Pamela Martin, and Martyn and Irene Kirby have provided invaluable help. Carl Ireland of Hull City Museums and Art Galleries has given much appreciated help by providing details of cars and their owners. I should be very grateful for any further information from readers who recognise scenes so far unidentified or who have evidence that the captions used are incorrect.
 One clear moral emerges: all photographs should be accurately labelled!

J.M.

Acknowledgements
Grateful thanks are recorded to Humberside Libraries and Arts for permission to reproduce illustrations of Squire William Draper, Thomas Hodgson, James Middleton Hall, and Arthur Wilson from the volume, *Sketches of Beverley and the Neighbourhood*, in the collection of the Beverley Reference Library.
 The staffs of the Beverley Reference Library and the Hull Local Studies Library have once again been most helpful and cooperative while work has been in progress on this book.

Squire William Draper of Beswick Hall, a great hunter in the 18th century. [Humberside Libraries and Arts]

The Holderness Hunt

An Introduction
by John Markham

The photographs in this book, showing the Holderness Hunt in the Edwardian period, are taken from a collection of over 340 purchased from Michael Kemp of the Cottingham Book Shop, after attention had been drawn to them by Christopher Ketchell of the Local History Archives Unit, who considered their quantity and quality made them a historical source too important to leave the area where they possessed the greatest interest. Mr. Kemp had bought them from another bookseller who in turn had purchased them at an auction in the North.

So far the original owner of the photographs has not been identified but it was possibly a prominent member of East Riding society at the turn of the century, or even the photographer himself. Some are stamped 'T. Tanfield, Beverley', who directories show was a cycle agent of 6 Wednesday Market but who must have been a photographer of considerable skill. A few carry a date, and even fewer name the scene.

The photographs provide a rare and probably unique picture of one aspect of Edwardian rural life. What emerges beyond any doubt is the enormous interest fox hunting aroused and the prominent role it played in the countryside. A meet was an eagerly anticipated event with non-riders far outnumbering the mounted followers. By the 19th century hunting was 'woven inseparably' into the pattern of country life and there were few who could imagine rural England without it. 'M.F.H.' after one's name could induce more respect than the letters 'M.P.', and the colourful and lively atmosphere of a meet attracted women and children and provided an irresistible temptation to men who should have been at work but who followed the hunt on foot over incredible distances.

It was a sport which brought together a remarkably varied cross-section of the local population, though the leading figures in the hunt were those in the upper échelons of society. Hunting enabled social climbers to mix with those they aspired to join, but the geographical isolation of Holderness probably meant that the hunt there remained traditionally 'county' when more fashionable hunts in the south had been infiltrated by newcomers.

What made hunting unique was the paradox at its heart: an aristocratic sport, it had enormous popular appeal. It gave country people of all types and classes the opportunity to rub shoulders — sometimes literally — with each other, and it fostered a strong sense of community and common interest and so strengthened the comforting feeling of stability in which most people liked to believe. 'Fox hunting,' one Holderness author wrote, 'is for all, from prince to peasant, duke to chimney-sweep, saint to sinner, the millionaire on his five-hundred-guinea hunter to the coster on his ten-shilling donkey, in fact the hunting field is open gratuitously to every class of man, the sole requisite being the ability to beg, borrow, buy or steal one animal with four legs to sit across.'

The Early Years: Thomas Hodgson

In the years covered by the photographs, the Edwardian period, the Holderness Hunt had reached a social eminence which was never quite recaptured after the First World War.

It was a glamorous epoch, the culmination of events dating back to the early 19th century. Although hunting in Holderness has a long recorded history, with Edward I granting a licence in 1279 to Adam de Everingham to hunt the king's chases and forests of Holderness, and with disputes over the claims of Archbishops of York to hunt the Westwood forming a significant chapter in the story of mediaeval Beverley, it was only in 1824 that the palmy days of the Holderness began. There had been the heroic days of Squire Draper of Beswick Hall in the 17th century, and a number of famous Yorkshire families were represented in the Georgian hunting field by such devotees as Humphrey Osbaldeston of Hunmanby, Lord Feversham, William Bethell of Rise, Sir Tatton and Sir Mark Masterman Sykes, Digby Legard and Richard Watts.

But in 1824 one of the legendary Yorkshire characters, Thomas Hodgson, became Master of the Holderness, and Beverley, which he made his base, developed as the hunting centre of the area with monthly meetings of the Hunt Club, founded in 1828 at the Tiger Inn. Dinner was followed by a ball at the Assembly Rooms and hunting provided the focal point of a hectic social life: 'Beverley has never known such a time before or since, for strangers came to winter there as well as the gentlemen of the county.'

Although Hodgson was surrounded by the wealthy and the privileged, his own means were modest. For a time he lived at the Rose and Crown in such a meagre style that apparently he could sit on his bed, stir the fire, and see his hounds through a hole in the wall — all at the same time. Eventually he settled at Bishop Burton and kept his hounds in what is still known as Dog Kennel Lane. Rather out of character for a man who 'lived only for hunting', in 1842 he was elected Registrar of Deeds for the West Riding.

James Middleton Hall

Five years later, a man of different type and background, James Middleton Hall, the squire of Scorborough, began a 30-year mastership of the hunt.

Nationally, this was a period of agricultural prosperity and 'high farming', and for hunting it was a golden age. The pessimists who had prophesied that railways would be the death of hunting were confounded. Railways did *not* ruin hunting country, as forecast, but, instead, enabled hunters, horses and hounds to move easily and quickly over greater distances: the Holderness was using the railway as early as 1846. Hunting became more popular and more fashionable and acquired greater prestige. The Holderness could not claim the status of more famous, better located hunts, but, even so, it was estimated that the number who hunted with the Holderness increased ten-fold in the 30 years 1843-73.

James Middleton Hall, grandson of William Middleton, the Georgian builder who contributed so much to the character and appearance of Beverley, and son of a man

Thomas Hodgson, 17 years Master of the Holderness.   [Humberside Libraries and Arts]

who became mayor of the town, was born in 1801. In 1833 he married Sarah, eldest daughter of Richard Watt of Bishop Burton, a union which resulted two generations later in the renamed Hall Watts. By profession a senior partner in the East Riding Bank in Beverley, his lineage was less distinguished that that of his hounds and horses where he demanded breeding of the highest standards. His ancestry nevertheless demonstrated the flexibility of English society and the opportunities open to men of ability to raise their social status.

Hall's paternal great-grandfather is said to have been a Swanland wheelwright, his grandfather a house servant for Lord Hotham, and his father steward for the same family. James had achieved a higher rank as agent for the Hothams' Yorkshire estates and he also farmed on his own account in a substantial way.

Following Lord Hotham's example at South Dalton, he employed the renowned architect, J. L. Pearson, to design a new church for Scorborough, in similar style though, with due deference to rank, not as grand as the one built for his lordship. It was opened with great jubilation, marquees were erected in the grounds of Scorborough Hall and food and drink were there for anyone who came.

In Hall's period as master the Holderness became 'one of the best mounted hunts in England'. His stud consisted of 46 horses, and Hall himself always rode a superb horse. Heavy clay and deep drains meant that 'only a well-bred horse can live with hounds in Holderness'.

Hall assumed without question the authority regarded as the birthright of a Yorkshire squire and he considered it only fitting that the vicar should await his arrival at church before beginning the service. One Sunday a relief parson began matins on time, annoying Hall who arrived late and found this egalitarian treatment offensive. 'Confound the man, couldn't he wait?' he stage whispered, loud enough for everyone in Scorborough church to hear.

He was the heroic figure of the kind the countryside admired. A breeder of prize-winning cattle and hounds and a fine judge of horses, he spoke his mind (or, as a more deferential age observed, was 'frank in utterance of his sentiments') and he was a generous, hospitable neighbour and spent the considerable sum of £600 each October keeping open house at Scorborough.

Hunting Parsons
During the 1860s the Holderness attracted a number of hunting parsons: these were the spacious days of the Anglican church when almost every tiny rural parish boasted its own resident clergyman, usually an Oxbridge graduate, who could find time hanging heavily on his hands unless he devoted himself to scholastic pursuits or the avocations of a country gentleman.

The most renowned of all the hunting parsons, Rev. John Bower, Rector of Brandesburton, comes earlier in the annals of the Holderness: 'He was not a clever man, or an inspiring preacher, but his people honoured and loved him beyond measure, because they knew him to be the best and hardest rider in the three Ridings.'

The local list of hunting parsons in the high Victorian period included Hall's son-

James Middleton Hall, Master of the Holderness 1847-77.   [Humberside Libraries and Arts]

in-law, Rev. Cecil Legard, Rector of Boynton ('not only a pillar of the Church but also in the hunting field'); Rev. Charles Atkinson, Rector of Harswell ('a dearly-loved clergyman and a very good man to hounds'); Rev. J. P. Seabrook, curate of Burton Agnes (who once caused a funeral to be delayed when the hunt had led him miles from his parish but was excused by one of the bereaved who 'knew that he had been profitably delayed, and, as he remarked on such a morning, "It was good keeping weather." '); and Rev. W. H. Higgens.

Lady Riders, Farmers and the Gentry

The pictures which follow prove how popular the hunt was with women — or more properly, 'ladies' — in the Edwardian period. In the early 19th century few females rode to hounds but their numbers had been growing from mid-century. Two of James Hall's daughters were noted hunters, Emily, who became Mrs. Cecil Legard, and Frances known as 'Miss Pop' in the Holderness field, whom no one could overtake 'even though the fences were as big as fortifications'; presumably she earned her nickname by going off with speed and thrust of a champagne cork.

Other well-known lady riders were likewise members of country families brought up in an environment where hunting was one of the principal reasons for living and summer, not winter, was the dreadful season of discontent. Prominent were three daughters of the appropriately named Charles Reynard, who lived for a time at Norwood House, Beverley; after marriage they became the Mesdames Clarke, Key and Slingsby. There were also the two sisters of William Bethell of Rise, and Miss L'Estrange (later Lady Erroll) who 'was a constant follower of hounds' when staying at Warter Priory with her sister, Lady Muncaster.

Hunting relied — and relies — on the goodwill of the local farmers; both in the days of prosperity and in the later periods of agricultural depression a number of substantial farmers followed the Holderness on their well-bred mounts. Those who did not ride to hounds were usually 'kindly disposed to the pack' and a later Master, Arthur Wilson, lauded them as 'the best lot of sporting farmers in England'.

Another paradox of hunting was its aid to conservation. Farmers who were friendly to the hunt helped to preserve foxes by ensuring that their earths were not disturbed and by planting or protecting coverts where they could breed. In 1951 the distinguished local historian, K. A. MacMahon, investigated a field belonging to Mr. John Dunning of Cold Harbour Farm, Bishop Burton, known as Fox Cover. Quantities of bricks and stones were being turned up by the plough, and Mr. MacMahon's opinion was that this had been an artificial fox earth, probably dating from the Georgian period.

Superior to the farmers in rank were such county notables as Lord Herries, Sir Henry Boynton and the two M.P.s for the East Riding, Christopher Sykes of Brantinghamthorpe and William Henry Harrison-Broadley of Welton House. Sykes, a tall and stooping figure, was 'an indifferent horseman', whose 'length of leg was rather against him, as his toes used to catch in the fence and upset his somewhat weak seat', though his horses were of the same high quality as those of Harrison-Broadley, who in his younger days had been 'quite an average man over a country but by no means a thruster'. There was a memorable occasion which caused great hilarity to spectators when the two M.P.s were stranded together in one of Holderness's formidable drains. History does not record who was the first to escape.

When James Hall had been Master for ten years a celebratory dinner in his honour was held on 18 November 1857 in the Assembly Rooms, Beverley, which his maternal grandfather, William Middleton, had built. As a token of esteem his friends and admirers presented him with his portrait, painted by Sir Francis Grant, and a set of 48 silver dinner plates and 18 soup plates. While the gentlemen banqueted and speechified in the Assembly Rooms, Mrs. Hall and the ladies held their own dinner next door at Norwood House.

Arthur Wilson

James Hall died in 1877, and one year later began an equally significant chapter: the 27-year mastership of Arthur Wilson of Tranby Croft.

He was a man of considerable wealth, a modern merchant prince, a member of the Hull family which ultimately owned the largest private shipping fleet in the world. His appointment as master was nevertheless evidence of social change. This was not a man descended from a long-established landed family, not even, like James Hall, with rural roots, but one whose wealth depended, quite literally, upon trade. He had not been a particularly keen hunter, but his acceptance of the mastership was itself an indication of the honoured status bestowed by the designation 'M.F.H.'.

Wilson's background may have differed from Hall's but he was the right man for the time, 'quiet and courteous in the field', and he was not merely respected but soon regarded with real affection through the Holderness countryside. He quickly made up for his late development as a hunter by a newly-acquired enthusiasm which gathered momentum the more he participated: 'No day is too rough, no distance too far to stop his going out; no time in the afternoon too late so long as there is light for this keen sportsman; and his endeavour is to show sport and get the hounds well away, and he is well supported by a keen but thoroughly sportsmanlike field.'

Wilson hunted 'in lavish style', buying the best-bred horses for his servants as well as himself and so earned the favourable opinion of the local farmers who were happy to supply them.

Royal Patronage

The reputation of the Holderness reached its zenith when it received royal recognition in the overweight form of the Prince of Wales, the future Edward VII, who came to the East Riding as the honoured, though appallingly behaved, friend of Christopher Sykes M.P. On 27 January 1882 the Hunt met in an idyllic setting at Brantinghamthorpe where every selfish whim of the royal guest was being instantly gratified.

It was a colourful, magnificent scene, the epitome of hunting, bringing together representatives of every strata of the local community: 'An immense concourse of people gathered together, and never within the memory of the oldest member of the hunt had such a meet been witnessed: high and low, rich and poor, peer and costermonger, all turning out to do honour to the Prince.' Crowd estimates are notoriously inaccurate but the count of about 1,400 on horse-back, 1,000 in carriages, with those on foot making a grand total of 4,000, may be reasonably near the truth. The local gentry and aristocracy turned out in force, among them Lord Herries, Lord Wenlock, W. H. Harrison-Broadley M.P. and Sir George Wombwell, along with members of neighbouring hunts: 'The spectacle in front of the house was quite unprecedented in the annals of the chase; and when His Royal Highness came out upon the terrace, the cheers that rent the air must have echoed in every valley of the district, and wakened many a dormant "Charlie" from his sweet reponse.' After such a brilliant start it was perhaps inevitable that the rest of the day should seem an anticlimax and it must have been a hard struggle to pretend that the dense fog which descended had not rather spoilt the fun.

The Prince's elder son, Prince Albert Victor, a dissolute young man who, if he had lived, would, incongruously, have been the husband of the future Queen Mary, also patronised the Hunt. On 18 January 1888 he attended the Hunt Ball and, after hunting the following day, attended another ball, at Tranby Croft, and on 21 January he was present at the meet at White Cross, Leven. He was out with the Holderness again in 1891.

Edwardian Hunters
Most of the Wilson family were keen hunters. Arthur's son, Clive, and his great-grandson, James, both followed him as Masters of the Holderness. His son-in-law, Edward Lycett-Green was Master of the York and Ainsty Hounds, and his grandson, Arthur Wilson-Filmer, was chairman of the Holderness and one of its most generous supporters. The Wilson ladies also added fashion and beauty to the Hunt, among them Mrs. Wilson and her daughters, Mrs. John G. Menzies. Mrs. Edward Lycett-Green and Muriel (later Mrs. Richard Warde), along with the daughters of Arthur's brother, Charles, Lady Cowley and Lady Chesterfield. From other eminent local families came Lady Boynton, and her daughter, Cycely (later Mrs. T. Wickham-Boynton), Jessica Sykes, the high-spirited wife of the introverted fifth baronet, Sir Tatton, and three daughters of Henry Constable of Wassand. At a time when women were regarded as inferiors at the polling booths, they proved themselves the equals, and sometimes the superiors, of men in the hunting field. One of them, Miss Wade (later Mrs. Leonard Pease), would not have tolerated discrimination: 'Drains have no terror for her. If not over them — then in, and chance getting out.'

Towards the end of Arthur Wilson's mastership on 12 January 1904 Lord Herries took the chair at a banquet held at the Public Rooms (now the New Theatre) in Hull, at which Wilson was presented with his portrait in oils as a small testimonial from the followers of the Holderness 'for the admirable way in which, for 25 seasons, he had carried on and preserved the best hunting traditions in the country.' It was a happy occasion, with Wilson recalling how, as a boy, he usually took a fall every day: 'If, however, he didn't get a fall one day, he invariably had two the next time he was out hunting so as not to spoil his average.'

Arthur Wilson, Master 1878-1905. [Humberside Libraries and Arts]

After Wilson
Arthur Wilson was a hard act to follow, but Charles Brook, owner of a Scottish estate, accepted the mastership in 1905, renting Cherry Burton Hall during the hunting season, though the demands on his attention from home compelled him to resign in 1908. Mr. H. Whitworth then came over from Ireland to be Master, renting James Hall's old home at Scorborough, 'which must have felt proud, after a lapse of 30 years, to once again house the Master of the Holderness'.

The Magic of Hunting
Arthur Wilson's mastership has been described by a famous Yorkshireman, Major J. Fairfax-Blakeborough, as the Holderness Hunt's most memorable and prosperous period when there was 'probably no happier hunt in the world'. The pictures in this book support that comment and suggest the cheerful atmosphere persisted in the years after Wilson's resignation.

Numerous films, television programmes and books have generated and helped to satisfy a nostalgia for Edwardian England, a time when the great country houses were expensively maintained and generously staffed, and their residents enjoyed a comfortable, traditional way of life which, they were fortunate not to realise, was on the verge of extinction. The outbreak of war in 1914 brought into being a different, more cruel world.

Edwardian England had its share of major social problems and these pictures convey only one facet of life. They are, nevertheless, a fascinating view of that facet of the social scene, quite apart from the hunting which brought them all together, though only a minority as participants.

Some of the meets were photographed in village centres, others on the lawns of the landed gentry, and a few are of the point-to-point. Their most striking feature is the massive interest aroused by the Hunt in people of all ages and types. Yet the riders, beautifully turned out and superbly mounted, seem to move on a far higher plain than the few feet separating than from the admiring crowd below and display a casual confidence in their superior position.

Bicycling was fashionable but the motorcar was a possession brought out proudly for public display. The odd proximity of constrasting forms of transport, animal and mechanical, was apparently taken for granted, though it symbolised a change which was to have profound consequences as the century progressed.

Above all, many of the photographs have extraordinary beauty. They have been taken by someone with an eye for the attractive shot which subtly but powerfully conveys an attitude or an atmosphere. The best are artistic compositions, as professional as stills from a sensitively directed film re-creating an idyllic vision of Edwardian England.

This may explain the intensity and the universality of the interest hunting aroused in country people. Possibly a desire to be part of something grander and more colourful than the petty greyness of everyday life was the powerful magnet which drew so many to the meets of the Holderness Hunt.

At Tranby Croft — the residence of Arthur Wilson

18 January 1907

At Tranby Croft

18 January 1907

At Tranby Croft

Arthur and Mary Wilson

18 January 1907

At Burton Constable Hall the residence of Major Walter Chichester-Constable

At Burton Constable Hall

At Welton House the residence of Colonel H. B. Harrison-Broadley

The Harrison-Broadleys were great supporters of the Holderness Hunt. Welton House was demolished in 1952.

The rider on the right (above) could be Colonel Henry Broadley Harrison-Broadley, M.P. for Howdenshire 1906-14.

At Welton House

At Cottingham

At Cottingham – Westfield House the residence of Mrs. Lambert (now Westfield Club)

At Cherry Burton Hall

Charles Brook, a Scottish landowner, rented Cherry Burton Hall during his mastership of the Holderness Hunt 1905-8.

At Burton Agnes Hall
the residence of Captain Thomas L. Wickham-Boynton

Lady Boynton and her daughter, Cycely, were enthusiastic followers of the Hunt. Cycely married Captain Thomas L. Wickham and the surname was then double-barrelled.

At White Cross, Leven the residence of the Misses Harrison

At Sunderlandwick Hall the (now demolished) residence of Frederick Reynard

Country Houses

Dalton Hall?

Country Houses

Country Houses

Village Scenes – at Newbald The Tiger Inn in background

Village Scenes – at Bishop Burton

A village with a long hunting history dating back at least to 1765 when William Bethell kept hounds there.

The Watts family of Bishop Burton were keenly interested in horses. Richard Watt's horse, Altisidora, won the St. Leger in 1813 and the village pub was renamed in its honour.

Village Scenes – at Bishop Burton

Village Scenes — at Beeford

The building in the background is the Tiger Inn, kept in the Edwardian period by Pexton Fowler.

Village Scenes – at Cranswick

Village Scenes – at Catwick

Village Scenes – at Catwick

Village Scenes

Village Scenes

At Wawne

At Wawne

Village Scenes – at Etton Kennels

The car, a dark green Vulcan with a side entrance (12-14 hp. 16 cwt.) was registered for tax on 31 August 1906 by Oswald F. Lambert, Westfield House, Cottingham, and later transferred to Alfred Smith, Hill Farm, Wawne.

Village Scenes – at Etton Kennels

Village Scenes – at Etton Kennels

Village Scenes – at Etton Kennels

At Beverley – Saturday Market

At Beverley – Saturday Market

At Hedon – Market Hill

At Hedon – Market Hill

St. Augustine's church in background.

The Meet

The hounds arrive.

The Meet

The Meet

The Meet

The car, a Brougham-style brown Hotchkiss (24 hp. 37½ cwt) was registered on 11 November 1904 by Arthur Stanley Wilson of Raywell.

The Meet

The Meet

The Meet

'Fox hunting is for all, from prince to peasant, duke to chimney-sweep, saint to sinner, the millionaire on his five-hundred-guinea hunter to the coster-monger on his ten-shilling donkey...'

The Meet

The Meet

The Meet

The Meet

The Meet

The Meet

The Meet

The Meet

The Meet

The Meet

Tally-Ho!

Is this Beverley Station from an unusual angle?

Tally-Ho!

Tally-Ho!

Overcoming Obstacles

Crossing the River Hull by Wawne Ferry.

Overcoming Obstacles

63

In the Field

At the Point-to-Point — Burton Constable

The point-to-point is a major social event in East Yorkshire. Organised by the Holderness Hunt, it is now held each spring in Dalton Park.

At the Point-to-Point

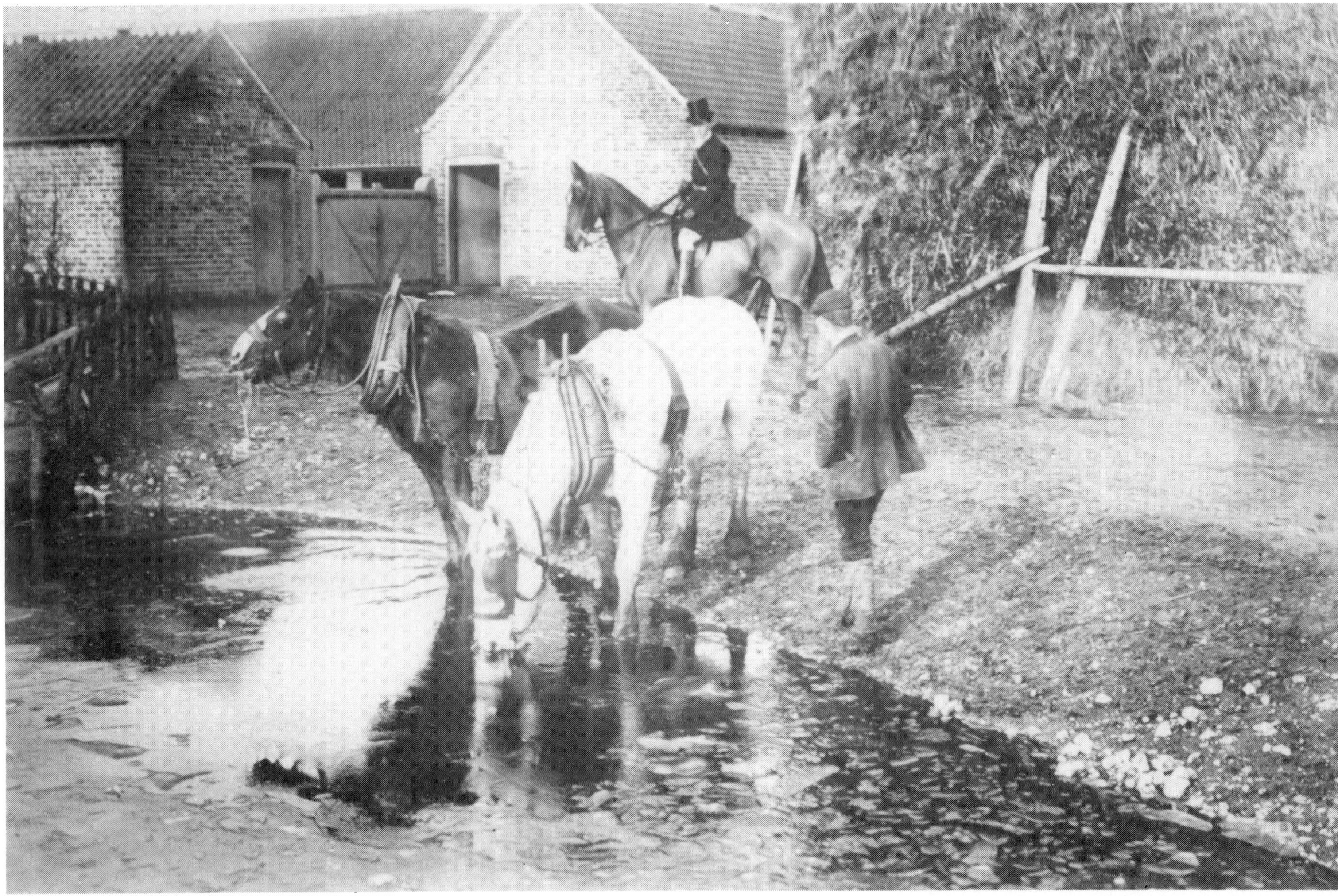